DORSET
IN PICTURES

MATTHEW PINNER

AMBERLEY

First published 2022

Amberley Publishing
The Hill, Stroud
Gloucestershire, GL5 4EP

www.amberley-books.com

Copyright © Matthew Pinner, 2022

The right of Matthew Pinner to be identified as the Author of this work has been asserted in accordance with the Copyrights, Designs and Patents Act 1988.

ISBN 978 1 3981 0693 2 (print)
ISBN 978 1 3981 0694 9 (ebook)

All rights reserved. No part of this book may be reprinted or reproduced or utilised in any form or by any electronic, mechanical or other means, now known or hereafter invented, including photocopying and recording, or in any information storage or retrieval system, without the permission in writing from the Publishers.

British Library Cataloguing in Publication Data.
A catalogue record for this book is available from the British Library.

Typesetting by SJmagic DESIGN SERVICES, India.
Printed in the UK.

ABOUT THE PHOTOGRAPHER

Matthew Pinner was born and raised for the early part of his life in the city of Southampton, Hampshire. After deciding at the age of twenty-two that he wanted to take up photography, he purchased his first camera after being left a tripod by his grandfather. It was his mission to learn everything he could by himself.

Matt's gallery of work is constantly expanding along with the requests for a book of his work. The inspiration behind this book is to showcase the pure beauty of the county of Dorset, which has been a massive part of his childhood, along with the amazing support of his mass social media following which reaches over 400,000 followers.

Matt's eight-year photography career has seen him achieve so much in such a short time. Many major TV outlets, newspapers and magazines have regularly asked to use his spectacular images nationally, to best represent the UK landscapes.

Matt uses a Canon 5D Mark IV with a range of lenses by Canon and he uses a wide range of filters by Lee Filters.

Website: http://pinners-photography.co.uk
Facebook: Pinner's Photography
Twitter: @Matt_Pinner
Instagram: @Matt_Pinner
Email: enquiriespinnersphotogrpahy@gmail.co.uk

ACKNOWLEDGEMENTS

I would like to start by saying that I am entirely grateful to so many of the people who are close to me for supporting me whist creating this book. First and most important is my beautiful wife, Emma, and our daughters Imogen and Sienna. You three have been my rock through this process and I love you very much.

There are also many members within the industry who have supported and guided me that I would like to do a special mention. Canon UK & Ireland, Angela Nicholson from *Camera Jabber*, Dean Murray from *Cover Images*, the people from *Bournemouth Echo*, Holly Green from *ITV weather*, Elliot Wagland, John Challis, *Dorset Magazine*, Paul Vass, Gareth Richman and Elie Gordon from *BBC Earth*.

INTRODUCTION

I first became interested in photography after my grandfather sadly passed away, leaving his tripod in his will for me. I found the inspiration from there and have never looked back. I live by the saying 'you miss every shot you don't take'. With every chance I get I'm constantly researching the next place to capture with my camera, and when I'm free to explore I'm gone roaming around the UK's southern coast to capture as many images as I possibly can.

 All the images within this book have been collected mainly over the last year; with taking these images I have been exploring as much as the county of Dorset as I possibly could, and within that I have chosen the ones that mean something to myself. The images are a continuation from my last book, *Dorset in Photographs*, that show other aspects of our gorgeous coastline.

 I love photography so much and I enjoy sharing the magical views I see in the early hours and last minutes of the day. I hope you enjoy the book as much as I enjoyed creating it.

The Castle Inn, Lulworth village

Sherborne Castle

Holy Trinity Church, Shaftesbury

Opium poppy field

Christchurch ruins

Tarrant Monkton

Fisherman's Bank, Mudeford

Highcliffe Castle

Gold Hill

Wild garlic woods

Corfe village

Cottages, near Abbotsbury

Sixpenny Handley

Abbotsbury

Lulworth Castle

Hardy's Monument

Fontmell Magna

Lulworth Ranges

Christchurch Bowling Green

Sculpture by the Lakes

St Mary's Church, Morden

Canford Magna School watermill

River Wareham

Bluebell Woods

Bat's Head

Highcliffe Beach

Cottage in Wool, near Wareham

Worth Matravers

Old Harry Rocks

Highcliffe Castle

Hengistbury Head

Southbourne

Hengistbury Head

Wimborne Minster

Boscombe Beach

Tyneham village church

Avon Beach

Thomas Hardy's Cottage

Knowlton Church

Okeford Fitzpaine

Chesil Beach

Grange Arch

Osmington Mills

Gold Hill

Ferne Park, near Shaftesbury

The Boathouse, Sherborne Castle

Lady Wimborne Bridge

Bournemouth Beach

Horton Tower

Win Green

Swanage Rail

Sixpenny Handley

Christchurch Priory

Ashmore Down

Winterborne Clenston

Cut Mill

Chapmans Pool

Alum Chine

Durlston Head Castle

St Michael & All Angels' Church, Littlebredy

Swyre Head

Swanage Pier

West Bay

Bournemouth Beach

Piddletrenthide village

Athelhampton House

Gold Hill in the snow

Badbury Rings

White Mill

Ferne Park, near Shaftesbury

Portland Bill

Tuckton, Christchurch

Steps to Man O'War Bay

Poppy field, near Forston

Old Swanage Pier

Lulworth village

Wild garlic

Little Waterfall, Osmington Mills

Mupe Bay

Bridport

Colmers Hill

Dungy Head

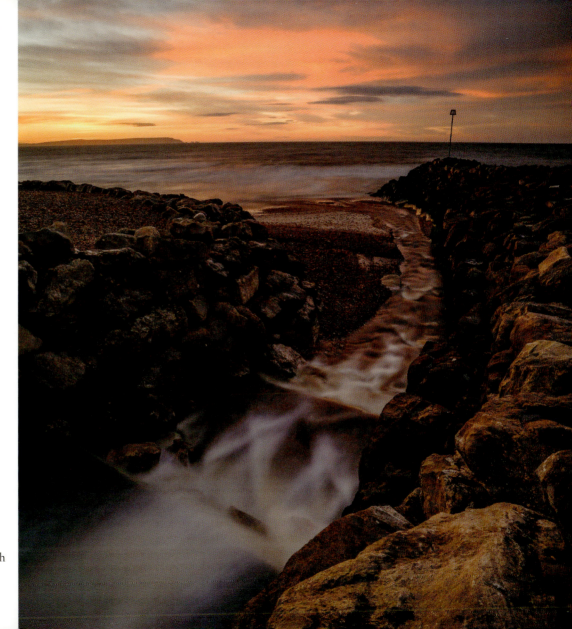

Highcliffe Beach

Wimborne Minster

Durdle Door

Kimmeridge

Bournemouth Pier

Corfe Castle

Ashmore Down

Horton Tower

Air show at Bournemouth Pier

The Three Legged Cross, Wimborne

Man O'War Bay

Hambledon Hill

Lulworth Cove

Hengistbury Head

Sculpture by the Lakes

Fontmell Magna

Old Quarry

Bournemouth Gardens

Knowlton Church

Worth Matravers

Shaftesbury town

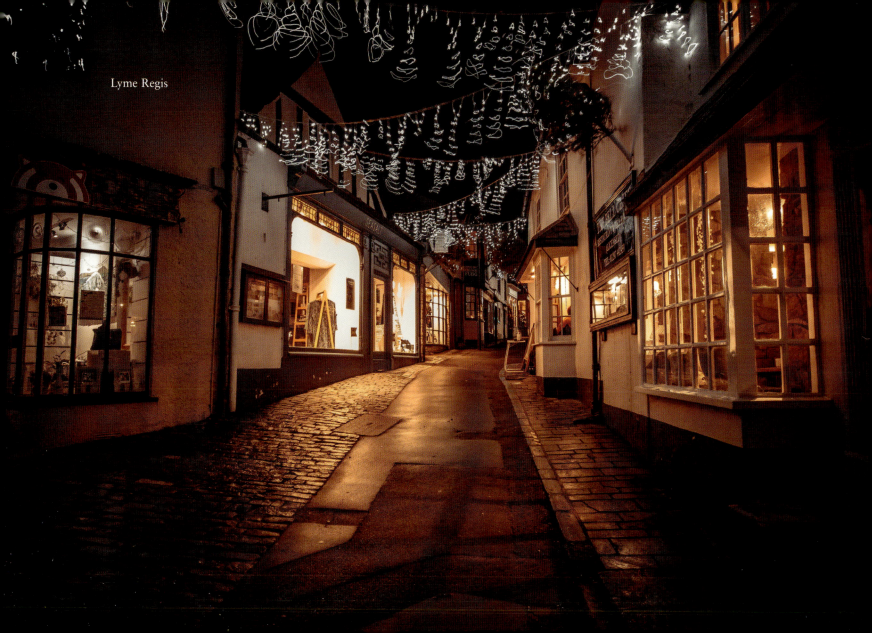

Lyme Regis

Chapmans Pool

Stair Hole

Sturminster Newton

Win Green

Milton Abbas

House in Lulworth village

House in Verwood

Field near Kingston Lacy

Sherborne Castle